Professional Cheerleading Audition Prep Workbook: A Companion Guide to the Audition Secrets Book

Flavia Berys

This workbook is a companion guide to the main book titled *Professional Cheerleading Audition Secrets: How To Become an Arena Cheerleader for NFL®, NBA®, and Other Pro Cheer Teams*.

This companion workbook should not be used alone, but only in conjunction with the main book. It is a step-by-step workbook that you can use to write down goals, ideas, and to track your progress. It has the checklists and worksheets you should use on your prep journey.

Additional copies available at www.ArenaCheerleader.com.

Published by

A Division of Cabri LLC
www.cabrimedia.com
Los Angeles County, California

Copyright © 2012-2013 Flavia Berys. All rights reserved.
No part of this work may be reproduced, published, or transmitted electronically without express written permission from the publisher.

First Printing, 2013
Printed in the United States of America

Photo credits:

Author headshot by Richard Pecjak, www.sunset-productions.com.

Book cover photo of the NBA Golden State Warrior Girl® (wearing white with blue and yellow accents, no sleeves) used with the permission of the Golden State Warriors, www.warriors.com. Photographer is Rey Jose II. The Warrior Girl cover model is Patrisha, who currently dances for the Golden State Warriors and has been a member of the team since the 2011 season. She is currently studying Public Relations. Her top audition tip is "To make sure when you audition that you dance full-out, have fun and perform with a lot of energy!"

Book cover photo of the NPSFL Enforcer Girl® (wearing red and black) used with the permission of the San Diego Enforcers, www.sandiegoenforcers.com. Photographer is Michael Manzano, www.manzanophotography.com. The Enforcer Girl cover model is Alexis Rodriguez, who currently dances for the San Diego Enforcers and is also the team's Dance Director. She works as an Admissions Operations Coordinator. Her top audition tip is "Have fun!"

Legal Notice & Disclaimer

Nothing contained in this book is to be considered medical, legal, or tax advice for your specific situation. The diet and nutrition information in this book has not been evaluated by the FDA and is not intended to treat, diagnose, cure or prevent any disease. This information is not intended as a substitute for the advice or medical care of your own physicians, attorneys, or tax advisors and you should consult with their own physicians, attorneys, or tax advisors prior to taking any personal action with respect to the information contained in this book. This book and all of its contents are intended for educational, entertainment and informational purposes only. The information in this book is believed to be reliable, but is presented without guaranty or warranty. By reading further, you agree to release the author and publisher from any damages or injury associated with your use of the material in this book. Some products mentioned in this book are under trademark or servicemark protection. Product and service names and terms are used only in an editorial fashion for educational purposes with no intent to infringe or dilute such trademarks. If links are provided to specific products, those links are for illustration purposes only and no warranty for such products or fitness for a particular purpose is implied. Such links may be affiliate links that compensate the publisher or author if a purchase is made through such link. Such products are available at a wide variety of retailers and no recommendation is made or implied to use any particular retailer. The opinions of the author do not necessarily reflect the opinions of the publisher.

About the Author

Flavia Berys is an experienced judge and organizer for professional cheerleading auditions worldwide. *The Wall Street Journal*, Fox 6 San Diego, KFMB Channel 8 San Diego, *Muscle & Fitness Magazine*, *Woman's Digest*, *The La Jolla Light* and other media have featured stories about Flavia's involvement in the world of dance and cheerleading. Her 20-year involvement in the sport includes three years as a UCLA Cheerleader, five years as an instructor for the Universal Cheerleaders Association (UCA), and two years cheering professionally for the NFL as a San Diego Charger Girl before taking her cheerleading career behind the scenes. Flavia coordinated the promotional appearances and transportation logistics for the 2002 and 2003 NFL Pro Bowl cheerleading programs in Honolulu, Hawaii, where she had the opportunity to meet and work with cheerleaders from almost every NFL football team as an Associate Producer for e2k Sports. She was also hired by e2k sports to direct the San Diego Sockers Performance Team, a professional co-ed stunt squad, for two seasons. Flavia also directed and choreographed the halftime shows for the 2000, 2001, and 2002 San Diego Jr. Charger Girl Programs, and organized and administered a series of youth cheerleading clinics on the island of Guam. She was contracted by e2k Sports to travel internationally to Prague, Czech Republic, where she directed Eastern Europe's first professional cheerleading team, the Eurotel Cheerleaders, which was later renamed the Chilli Cheerleaders. She serves as the executive advisor to professional cheerleading teams such as the San Diego Enforcer Girls in the NPSFL football league. She has worked as an expert witness for trials involving cheerleading negligence litigation, and is the author of other upcoming cheerleading books, *Pom Poms in Prague: A True Story* and *Professional Cheerleading: A Director's Guide to Starting, Managing, and Marketing an Arena Cheerleader Dance Team*. Aside from her cheer-related career, Flavia is an attorney, business coach, and real estate broker. She teaches as an adjunct professor at California Western School of Law and San Diego City College. Flavia is available as a motivational speaker and executive consultant. Connect with her at flavia@berys.com.

How to Use This Workbook

If you are holding this workbook, then you have already read (or are currently reading) the main book, *Professional Cheerleading Audition Secrets: How To Become an Arena Cheerleader for NFL®, NBA®, and Other Pro Cheer Teams*.

This means you understand that preparation is key, and procrastination is the enemy.

I have developed this workbook to track the contents of the main book, chapter by chapter, giving you a place to journal, dream, take notes, and track your improvement.

In my dreams, you will transform this crisp, new workbook into a dog-eared, well-worn memento that is not only a tool for you, but also a memory book. The only way this workbook will work is if you use it consistently.

My own dreams for this project will come true if you and the other readers use this book to succeed in your goals to become arena cheerleaders. I want this workbook to make its way into your memory-box, which will also hold photographs, team posters, calendars, pom-poms, souvenirs, notes from team members, and other keepsakes from your pro cheerleading career.

I want this workbook to be the catalyst that springboards you to success.

Let's begin!

IS THIS SPORT FOR YOU?

Why do you want to become a professional cheerleader?

In the book, I described the many ways that pro cheerleading can bring great things into your life. Take a few moments to analyze your own personal motivations, and write them down below. I have also included the list from the main book, so feel free to circle as many of those that apply to you. Remember, be honest with yourself about your own personal reasons. And add any that I did not mention in the book, such as (for example) "To follow in my big sister's footsteps because she was a Teamname cheerleader" or "To make my dad proud, because he is a huge Teamname fan."

Fun & Excitement
Glamour
Camaraderie & Friendships
Contacts & Networking
Resume Building
Media & Entertainment Opportunities
Confidence Building
Personal Growth & Achievement

Your notes:_____
_____
_____
_____
_____
_____
_____
_____

Are you the ideal pro cheerleader "type"?

Ask yourself:	Answer honestly:	Notes & goals:
Do you love sports?	☐ Yes ☐ No, but I will ☐ No	_____
Do you have dance training?	☐ Yes ☐ No, but I will ☐ No	_____
Do you have a "team" attitude rather than a "me" attitude?	☐ Yes ☐ No, but I will ☐ No	_____
Are you physically fit and athletic?	☐ Yes ☐ No, but I will ☐ No	_____
Do you have a polished look or are you interested in getting more polished?	☐ Yes ☐ No, but I will ☐ No	_____
Are you well spoken with good manners?	☐ Yes ☐ No, but I will ☐ No	_____
Do you have a natural energy that people around you respond to?	☐ Yes ☐ No, but I will ☐ No	_____
Do you have enough free time to commit to the game and promotional schedule this sport demands?	☐ Yes ☐ No, but I will ☐ No	_____
Are you at least 18 years old?	☐ Yes ☐ No, but I will ☐ No	_____

Read your answers to the questions above. Are they mostly "yes"? Are most of your "no" answers "no, but I will"? And which areas of your life need change? Make good notes about your thoughts and goals for these areas of your life. If this is your goal, you will need to make changes in any area where the answer wasn't "yes."

What are the three biggest common myths about looks, body type, and diversity?

Which of these myths did you believe before? And what did you learn from the main book that helped you emotionally or mentally? Was it a relief to hear some of these answers, even if you already suspected these were just myths?

Myth #1: You have to be "model" gorgeous
Truth: Looks matter, but not as much as you might think

Your thoughts:_____
_____
_____
_____
_____
_____
_____
_____
_____

Myth #2: You have to be practically anorexic and "skeleton" skinny
Truth: Being skinny and skeletal is not the body-type goal

Your thoughts:_____
_____
_____
_____
_____
_____
_____
_____
_____

Myth #3: Teams have "diversity quotas" for minority applicants
Truth: Teams do not discriminate by giving or deducting points solely for diversity

Your thoughts:_____
_____
_____
_____
_____
_____
_____
_____
_____

Professional Cheerleading Audition Prep Workbook: A Companion Guide to the Audition Secrets Book
For **Bonus Material**, join the Arena Cheer community at www.ArenaCheerleader.com

Your Journaling and Notes:

YOUR RESEARCH & ADVANCE PREP

Let's get you prepared for auditions!

What's your most dangerous audition success enemy? Procrastination!

Are you a procrastinator by nature? ❏Yes, always   ❏Yes, sometimes   ❏No

If you answered "yes" or "yes, sometimes," what are some ways you will personally fight procrastination? Make those commitments now, in writing, by making statements about how you will change your behavior. Remember, this is a contract with yourself, so take these promises seriously. Write your statements down in a tone that means business!

Your thoughts:_____
_____
_____
_____
_____

Your promises to yourself and commitments:_____
_____
_____
_____
_____
_____

Here's your research checklist and workbook!

Why am I asking you to write these items down? Because that way you can't put it off. If I ask you to actually TELL me which calendar you will use to track important dates, that forces you to designate a specific calendar and moves that item from "will do" to "DONE"!

- ✓ **Create a research binder.** What have you decided to use? A three-ring binder? A computer folder online? A shoebox? Write down what you are using here:
  _____

- ✓ **Make a calendar.** What have you decided to use? A wall calendar? A day planner? An online computer calendar? Write down what you are using here:
  _____
  Where do you keep that calendar?_____

- ✓ **Research local teams.**
  Without narrowing the list only to the teams you will audition for, what are all the local professional cheerleading and dance teams in your nearby area?
  _____
  _____
  _____
  _____
  _____
  Don't forget to consider non-NFL or NBA teams as well!

- ✓ **Research non-local teams.**
  Which are the non-local teams that you would be willing to move for if you made the team? Include the name of the city when you name the team.
  _____
  _____
  _____
  _____
  _____
  Again, don't forget to consider non-NFL or NBA teams as well!

- ✓ **Compile.** For each team you identify above, visit their web page and print out or cut and paste all relevant info about the cheerleading program into your research file. Create a separate section for each team. You should include the following, if available online. You can use the grid below to help you organize your research.

Your top 10 teams that you are researching:

1. _____
2. _____
3. _____
4. _____
5. _____
6. _____
7. _____
8. _____
9. _____
10. _____

Research task:	Task complete for these teams:		Notes:
General information about the sports organization, such as where they play and which league they play for.	☐ Team #1 ☐ Team #2 ☐ Team #3 ☐ Team #4 ☐ Team #5	☐ Team #6 ☐ Team #7 ☐ Team #8 ☐ Team #9 ☐ Team #10	_____
Photos of the current dance team, especially the team photo.	☐ Team #1 ☐ Team #2 ☐ Team #3 ☐ Team #4 ☐ Team #5	☐ Team #6 ☐ Team #7 ☐ Team #8 ☐ Team #9 ☐ Team #10	_____
Individual photos of the dance team members.	☐ Team #1 ☐ Team #2 ☐ Team #3 ☐ Team #4 ☐ Team #5	☐ Team #6 ☐ Team #7 ☐ Team #8 ☐ Team #9 ☐ Team #10	_____
Sample biography pages of the dance team members.	☐ Team #1 ☐ Team #2 ☐ Team #3 ☐ Team #4 ☐ Team #5	☐ Team #6 ☐ Team #7 ☐ Team #8 ☐ Team #9 ☐ Team #10	_____
Information about dance team auditions, including any handouts or applications that you can download.	☐ Team #1 ☐ Team #2 ☐ Team #3 ☐ Team #4 ☐ Team #5	☐ Team #6 ☐ Team #7 ☐ Team #8 ☐ Team #9 ☐ Team #10	_____
General information about the dance team, such as how many members are on it and how often they rehearse.	☐ Team #1 ☐ Team #2 ☐ Team #3 ☐ Team #4 ☐ Team #5	☐ Team #6 ☐ Team #7 ☐ Team #8 ☐ Team #9 ☐ Team #10	_____

Task			Notes
Contact information for the team director and/or coach.	☐ Team #1 ☐ Team #2 ☐ Team #3 ☐ Team #4 ☐ Team #5	☐ Team #6 ☐ Team #7 ☐ Team #8 ☐ Team #9 ☐ Team #10	_____ _____ _____ _____ _____
Information about any team-sponsored dance workshops or meetings.	☐ Team #1 ☐ Team #2 ☐ Team #3 ☐ Team #4 ☐ Team #5	☐ Team #6 ☐ Team #7 ☐ Team #8 ☐ Team #9 ☐ Team #10	_____ _____ _____ _____ _____
Season schedule, or range of months if the exact game schedule is not available.	☐ Team #1 ☐ Team #2 ☐ Team #3 ☐ Team #4 ☐ Team #5	☐ Team #6 ☐ Team #7 ☐ Team #8 ☐ Team #9 ☐ Team #10	_____ _____ _____ _____ _____
Watch all videos available on Youtube® or on the team website that showcase the dance team, and make notes about the dance style and level of difficulty.	☐ Team #1 ☐ Team #2 ☐ Team #3 ☐ Team #4 ☐ Team #5	☐ Team #6 ☐ Team #7 ☐ Team #8 ☐ Team #9 ☐ Team #10	_____ _____ _____ _____ _____
Make a note about whether each team uses pom-poms or not. If poms are used, research to see if you will need to use pom-poms at the audition.	☐ Team #1 ☐ Team #2 ☐ Team #3 ☐ Team #4 ☐ Team #5	☐ Team #6 ☐ Team #7 ☐ Team #8 ☐ Team #9 ☐ Team #10	_____ _____ _____ _____ _____
Run a Google® search on each team two ways: First, run a standard search. Then, run an "image" search. Read press releases and articles, and review images that come up on the search.	☐ Team #1 ☐ Team #2 ☐ Team #3 ☐ Team #4 ☐ Team #5	☐ Team #6 ☐ Team #7 ☐ Team #8 ☐ Team #9 ☐ Team #10	_____ _____ _____ _____ _____

- ❏ **Contact team directors.** There are sample scripts to use in the main book, and some tips for how to reach out to team management in a way that will help your audition efforts. Check this box off once you have contacted as many directors as you are able to reach.
    - ❏ Team #1 ❏ Team #6   Notes:
    - ❏ Team #2 ❏ Team #7
    - ❏ Team #3 ❏ Team #8
    - ❏ Team #4 ❏ Team #9
    - ❏ Team #5 ❏ Team #10

- ❏ **Fill in your calendar.** As you compile the information above, enter any relevant dates and deadlines into your calendar. If you are interested in many different teams, it might be helpful to color-code your calendar entries. Enter season start dates, games, audition workshops, audition dates, bootcamp or mini-camp dates, rehearsal schedules, and any deadlines (such as application deadlines). This will help you determine which teams to focus on, since some auditions may occur on the same day or otherwise conflict. You can also see if it is possible to dance for more than one team, if the seasons do not overlap.

    For example, your calendar can include things like:
    - "Will try new tanning sprays this week."
    - "Try new dance classes this week to find best jazz and hip-hop instructors."
    - "Make hair appointment this month to try new color and cut."
    - "Go through Facebook® page and delete inappropriate photos."
    - "Find best self-tanner for my skin."
    - "Sign up for boot camp cross-training classes."
    - "Look through magazines to find good makeup looks."
    - "Sign up for Toastmasters® public speaking club."
    - "Experiment with ways to cover up tattoo."
    - "Start eating better this week; commit to maintaining a healthier diet starting now."
    - "Call dentists to find good deal on teeth bleaching; make appointment."
    - "Visit mall department store to experiment with lipstick colors."
    - "Practice applying false lashes."
    - "Need audition outfit by next week."
    - "Buy pom-poms online by today to begin practicing dancing with poms."
    - "Choreograph audition solo and 8-count this week."
    - "Videotape self doing solo routine; bring video to studio and ask dance teacher for feedback."
    - "Study football rules this week."
    - "Shopping list this week: Hosiery tights, false lashes and lash glue, and new dance shoes."

Obviously, this is only a sample list, but should give you an idea of the things you should calendar so that you stay on track and don't overlook something. You do not want to get caught off-guard racing around town to find the perfect dance shoes the night before auditions. Advance planning is key; it will help you focus on the important things the week of audition, like rehearsing your routine and getting lots of sleep, rather than shopping like a madwoman.

How sports savvy are you?

Do you need to work on your sports rules knowledge? If so, read a book about the sport's rules before you move on to the next step in this workbook.

❏ I can answer basic questions about the sports I would be cheering for.
❏ I need to read a book about the sport to learn the rules and terminology. I have ordered a book online or bought one in a book store and will have it finished by: ____/____/____.

Which skill areas need extra work?

My current skill level in each of these areas is:

Skill area:	My level of skill:	Notes:
Dance technique	Weak ❏1 ❏2 ❏3 ❏4 ❏5 Strong	
Showmanship	Weak ❏1 ❏2 ❏3 ❏4 ❏5 Strong	
Audition dance attire	Weak ❏1 ❏2 ❏3 ❏4 ❏5 Strong	
Fitness	Weak ❏1 ❏2 ❏3 ❏4 ❏5 Strong	

Nutrition & hydration	Weak ☐1 ☐2 ☐3 ☐4 ☐5 Strong	
Makeup	Weak ☐1 ☐2 ☐3 ☐4 ☐5 Strong	
Teeth	Weak ☐1 ☐2 ☐3 ☐4 ☐5 Strong	
Nails	Weak ☐1 ☐2 ☐3 ☐4 ☐5 Strong	
Skin (tattoo, acne, tanning, etc.)	Weak ☐1 ☐2 ☐3 ☐4 ☐5 Strong	
Hair cut	Weak ☐1 ☐2 ☐3 ☐4 ☐5 Strong	
Hair color	Weak ☐1 ☐2 ☐3 ☐4 ☐5 Strong	
Hairstyle	Weak ☐1 ☐2 ☐3 ☐4 ☐5 Strong	

Interview attire	Weak ☐1 ☐2 ☐3 ☐4 ☐5 Strong	_____
Confidence	Weak ☐1 ☐2 ☐3 ☐4 ☐5 Strong	_____
Motivation	Weak ☐1 ☐2 ☐3 ☐4 ☐5 Strong	_____
Dedication	Weak ☐1 ☐2 ☐3 ☐4 ☐5 Strong	_____
Sports knowledge	Weak ☐1 ☐2 ☐3 ☐4 ☐5 Strong	_____
Current events knowledge	Weak ☐1 ☐2 ☐3 ☐4 ☐5 Strong	_____
Team and league knowledge	Weak ☐1 ☐2 ☐3 ☐4 ☐5 Strong	_____

YOUR DANCING

Time to pick some dance styles you plan to practice!

- Arena dance.   ❏ Expert in this style ❏ Plan to take lessons
- Jazz.   ❏ Expert in this style ❏ Plan to take lessons
- Bellydance.   ❏ Expert in this style ❏ Plan to take lessons
- Latin ballroom styles. ❏ Expert in this style ❏ Plan to take lessons
- Hip-hop.   ❏ Expert in this style ❏ Plan to take lessons
- Bollywood.   ❏ Expert in this style ❏ Plan to take lessons
- Zumba®.   ❏ Expert in this style ❏ Plan to take lessons
- Broadway.   ❏ Expert in this style ❏ Plan to take lessons
- Disco.   ❏ Expert in this style ❏ Plan to take lessons

Less than ideal dance styles for arena cheerleading preparation (but still great add-ons as part of a well-rounded regime!):

- Ballet.   ❏ Expert in this style ❏ Plan to take lessons
- Modern.   ❏ Expert in this style ❏ Plan to take lessons
- Fitness aerobics.   ❏ Expert in this style ❏ Plan to take lessons
- Tap.   ❏ Expert in this style ❏ Plan to take lessons
- Yoga.   ❏ Expert in this style ❏ Plan to take lessons
- Hula.   ❏ Expert in this style ❏ Plan to take lessons
- Irish step dance.   ❏ Expert in this style ❏ Plan to take lessons
- Burlesque.   ❏ Expert in this style ❏ Plan to take lessons

Which classes (and at which studio) did you end up signing up for?
_____
_____
_____
_____

Do you have flexibility issues? If so, pick one of the styles below and begin attending at least twice per week to increase your flexibility.

- ☐ Yoga
- ☐ Classical ballet
- ☐ Hybrid ballet barre fitness classes
- ☐ Gymnastics
- ☐ Specialty stretching classes

Dance-related to-do items:

- ☐ Researched to see if any local dance teachers are pro cheerleaders
- ☐ Attended local workshops or audition prep bootcamps
- ☐ Attended larger regional bootcamp or retreat
- ☐ Choreographed a short 8-count that can be done during "freestyle" part
- ☐ Choreographed solo routine. My solo routine is (describe each 8-count):
  - 8-Count 1:_____
  - 8-Count 2:_____
  - 8-Count 3:_____
  - 8-Count 4:_____
  - 8-Count 5:_____
  - 8-Count 6:_____
  - 8-Count 7:_____
  - 8-Count 8:_____
  - 8-Count 9:_____
  - 8-Count 10:_____
  - 8-Count 11:_____
  - 8-Count 12:_____

Notes:_____
_____
_____
_____
_____
_____
_____
_____
_____
_____
_____
_____
_____

YOUR BODY

Evaluate your fitness level

In the main book, I explained that cheerleading is for fit, athletic women, not skinny undernourished waifs. This is a power sport, and to be powerful you need some muscles and lots of energy!

Fitness area:	My current level:	Notes & goals:
Energy burst (i.e., sprinting)	Weak ☐1 ☐2 ☐3 ☐4 ☐5 Strong	
Stamina (endurance)	Weak ☐1 ☐2 ☐3 ☐4 ☐5 Strong	
Cardio (do you get out of breathe easily?)	Weak ☐1 ☐2 ☐3 ☐4 ☐5 Strong	
Exercise regularly	Weak ☐1 ☐2 ☐3 ☐4 ☐5 Strong	

Muscle tone (also note whether one part of your body needs more work than others)	Weak ☐1 ☐2 ☐3 ☐4 ☐5 Strong	_____ _____ _____ _____ _____
Nutrition	Weak ☐1 ☐2 ☐3 ☐4 ☐5 Strong	_____ _____ _____ _____ _____
Hydration	Weak ☐1 ☐2 ☐3 ☐4 ☐5 Strong	_____ _____ _____ _____ _____

Your Journaling and Notes:

_____
_____
_____
_____
_____
_____
_____
_____
_____
_____
_____
_____
_____
_____
_____
_____
_____

YOUR GROOMING

What is the ideal "look" you will create?

This section is fun! The main book addresses grooming and appearance, so that you can develop the right look that judges will score highly on the day of tryouts.

In this section of the companion workbook, you can document the steps that you take. First, read the grooming section of the main book to learn how to define the right look. Then, come back to this companion workbook page to begin documenting your efforts!

Analyze the team photo for your target dream team. What do you notice about the team's makeup, hair, and accessories? What stands out to you about their "look"? Are most wearing larger fluffed-out hair and red lipstick? Or is the look "sleek" with straightened hair and softer makeup colors? Take a look and jot down your observations here!

Observations:_____
_____
_____
_____
_____
_____
_____
_____
_____
_____
_____
_____
_____
_____
_____
_____

Below, paste or staple sample photos taken from the team website or cut out of the team photo. You can find many images online. Focus on photos which show a team member who has a look you can replicate:

(Paste or staple images below)

Here is another page to use for your image gathering activity:

(Paste or staple images below - Continued)

What do you need to do to replicate your favorite target look?

First, write down the to-do item. Then, as you get each one done, check it off to track your progress!

To replicate my target "makeup" look, I need to:

1. _____ ❑Done!
2. _____ ❑Done!
3. _____ ❑Done!
4. _____ ❑Done!
5. _____ ❑Done!
6. _____ ❑Done!
7. _____ ❑Done!
8. _____ ❑Done!
9. _____ ❑Done!
10. _____ ❑Done!

To replicate my target "hairstyle" look, I need to:

1. _____ ❑Done!
2. _____ ❑Done!
3. _____ ❑Done!
4. _____ ❑Done!
5. _____ ❑Done!
6. _____ ❑Done!
7. _____ ❑Done!
8. _____ ❑Done!

To replicate my target "skin" look, I need to:

1. _____ ❑Done!
2. _____ ❑Done!
3. _____ ❑Done!
4. _____ ❑Done!
5. _____ ❑Done!

Miscellaneous (teeth, bra selection, cellulite treatment, contact lenses, nails, etc.) tasks:

1. _____ ❑Done!
2. _____ ❑Done!
3. _____ ❑Done!
4. _____ ❑Done!
5. _____ ❑Done!

YOUR AUDITION ATTIRE

What will your audition outfit be?

Now that your body, hair, and makeup looks are locked down, it's time to decide what you will wear for the dance and interview portions of the audition.

Ideas for a top:_____
_____
_____
_____
_____
_____
_____
_____

Ideas for your briefs:_____
_____
_____
_____
_____

Ideas for hosiery:_____
_____
_____
_____
_____

Ideas for your shoes:_____
_____

Below, paste or staple dance audition outfit ideas. You can find many images online.

(Paste or staple images below)

Photo shoot time!

When you obtain the dance outfit components, put them on and take some photos. Paste the photos below. If you have several different options you are comparing, wear each outfit and paste the photos below to be able to compare them.

(Paste or staple images below)

FINAL DANCE PORTION LOOK!

Once you have narrowed it down to your final dance portion look, take a final glamour shot and paste the photo below!

(Paste or staple your final audition look below)

What will your interview outfit be?

Just like you did for the dance outfit, it's time to generate ideas for the interview portion, then to narrow it down to a final choice.

Ideas for your interview outfit:_____
_____
_____
_____
_____
_____
_____
_____
_____
_____
_____
_____
_____
_____
_____
_____
_____
_____
_____

Ideas for your shoes:_____
_____
_____
_____
_____
_____

Ideas for your jewelry:_____
_____
_____
_____
_____

Misc. ideas:_____
_____
_____
_____

Below, paste or staple interview outfit ideas. You can find many images online.

(Paste or staple images below)

Photo shoot time for the interview outfit!

When you obtain the outfit components, put them on and take some photos. Paste the photos below. If you have several different options you are comparing, wear each outfit and paste the photos below to be able to compare them.

(Paste or staple images below)

FINAL INTERVIEW LOOK!

Once you have narrowed it down to your final interview portion look, take a glamour shot and paste the photo below!

```
(Paste or staple your final interview look below)
```

Don't forget to do the following:

1. Rehearse with your dance outfit on until you can dance in it easily ☐ Done!
2. Practice walking in your interview shoes until you do it with grace ☐ Done!
3. Practice sitting down and standing up in your interview outfit ☐ Done!
4. Practice dancing holding pom-poms in your dance outfit ☐ Done!

YOUR MINDSET & SELF

Reputation & image control

Don't forget to do the following:

1. Clean up your social media image (Facebook®, Twitter®, etc.) ☐Done!
2. Make amends with anyone you might have disappointed in the past ☐Done!
3. Practice interview questions until you can deliver them confidently ☐Done!
4. Review your research about the team, league, and current events ☐Done!
5. Upped your community involvement ☐Done!

Positive visualization: Use it!

The main book describes in detail some excellent exercises you can easily do to use positive visualization on your journey to becoming a professional cheerleader. Read the section on how to do each one, and then check them off as you complete them!

Dream board	☐ Done!	
Emotional tuning	☐ Started this process!	☐ Doing it regularly
Visualization	☐ Started this process!	☐ Doing it regularly
Affirmations	☐ Started this process!	☐ Doing it regularly

Using the sample affirmations presented in the main book as examples, create your OWN set of affirmations by writing them down on the following page in your own handwriting. Then, make photocopies of the page (or write out a copy by hand, which is even more effective) and pin copies to your wall, refrigerator, bathroom mirror, and anywhere else you can post it where you will see it on a regular basis.
Read them out often!

Your affirmations:

YOUR APPLICATION

Your application is important!

The main book gives you solid advice on how to fill out your application. Clip a copy of each application you submit to a team into this workbook. Just clip them all to this page to keep a record (and memory) of the contents of each application.

Include copies of any photos and headshots you submit, and a copy of any separate resume. Years from now, you will want to look back and read those applications and resumes! It's like a time capsule.

[Clip copies here]

YOUR AUDITION DAY

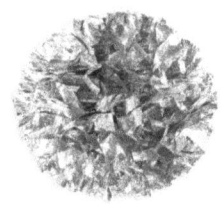

Audition Day Packing List

NOTE: Refer to the main book for a detailed description of the "Why?" and "How?" for each item below!

- ❒ Audition bag
- ❒ Small baggage lock
- ❒ Warm-ups
- ❒ Clear packing tape
- ❒ Safety pins
- ❒ Bottled water
- ❒ Snacks
- ❒ Mirror
- ❒ Makeup
- ❒ Hair tools and products
- ❒ Hot tool sleeve
- ❒ Tissues
- ❒ Backup outfit
- ❒ Hosiery
- ❒ Clear nail polish
- ❒ Toothbrush and toothpaste
- ❒ Deodorant
- ❒ Small towel
- ❒ Music
- ❒ Identification
- ❒ Cash
- ❒ Extra copy of your application
- ❒ Extra shoes
- ❒ Phone

Whom did you meet?

If you have this workbook with you on the day of your audition, jot down the names and contact information for friends you make.

Name	Phone	Email

Journal about how your day went:

Your thoughts:_____
_____
_____
_____
_____
_____
_____
_____
_____
_____
_____
_____
_____
_____
_____
_____
_____
_____
_____
_____
_____
_____

If you did not make the team, what will you work on to improve before your next audition?

Your thoughts:_____
_____
_____
_____
_____
_____
_____
_____
_____
_____
_____
_____
_____
_____
_____
_____
_____
_____
_____
_____
_____
_____
_____

If you made the team, congratulations!

Now be sure to mentor another aspiring pro dancer by helping her reach her dreams. Best wishes! You are now on your way to one of your life's most exciting adventures!

Much love,
Flavia

What next?

Visit the official website at www.ArenaCheerleader.com.

On the website, you can join the free mailing list to periodically receive:

- Choreography videos
- Tips & tricks
- Audition news
- Interviews with current pro cheerleaders
- Spotlight articles on team directors
- Announcements about new books and editions
- Info about retreats and bootcamps
- Discounts from companies who want you to try their makeup, nutrition, and other products
- Healthy recipes
- News and articles about the pro cheer world

Thanks again for purchasing this workbook and good luck at auditions!

Cheers!

www.ingramcontent.com/pod-product-compliance
Lightning Source LLC
Chambersburg PA
CBHW081025040426
42444CB00014B/3349